WATCHING FOR LIFE

THE HUGH MacLENNAN POETRY SERIES

Editors: Allan Hepburn and Carolyn Smart

TITLES IN THE SERIES

watching for life

DAVID ZIEROTH

McGill-Queen's University Press
Montreal & Kingston • London • Chicago

ISBN 978-0-2280-1474-4 (paper)
ISBN 978-0-2280-1591-8 (ePDF)
ISBN 978-0-2280-1592-5 (ePUB)

Legal deposit fourth quarter 2022
Bibliothèque nationale du Québec

Printed in Canada on acid-free paper that is 100% ancient forest free
(100% post-consumer recycled), processed chlorine free

We acknowledge the support of the Canada Council for the Arts.

Nous remercions le Conseil des arts du Canada de son soutien.

Library and Archives Canada Cataloguing in Publication

Title: Watching for life / David Zieroth.

Names: Zieroth, David, 1946- author.

Series: Hugh MacLennan poetry series.

Description: Series statement: The Hugh MacLennan poetry series

Identifiers: Canadiana (print) 2022028508X | Canadiana (ebook)
  20220285098 | ISBN 9780228014744 (softcover) |
  ISBN 9780228015918 (PDF) | ISBN 9780228015925 (ePUB)

Subjects: LCGFT: Poetry.

Classification: LCC PS8599.I47 W37 2022 | DDC C811/.54—DC23

This book was typeset by Marquis Interscript in 9.5/13 Sabon.

for Lucian, for Marlow

CONTENTS

WATCHING FOR LIFE

ON THE JOURNEY TOWARD
MY DEAD PARENTS

I have stopped here for a time, overlooking
this lane where strangers come and go
meaning nothing to me and yet welcome
as reminders that all of us have destinies
and days when what we do will not be
remembered, the forgotten time piling up
behind, which in retrospect seems a foolish
waste though not in the instant of being alive

and in this particular moment with no one
in view below I notice two large stones
by the entrance to the underground garage
and I wonder: were they dragged in from
a riverbed to stand as guards against cars
that want to leap out of their usual paths
in a hurry to descend to the half-lit world below
while out here these sentinels remain unmoved?
around their buried bases a scattering
of ornamental gravel white and unwilling
to allow any weeds to emerge

I wonder if these two grey rocks recall
the river they once knew, or if the river of cars
they now hear causes them any grieving
and further back still, do they remember at all
the molten magma out of which they came?
becoming individual and separate and with
no chance, not today anyway, to be shattered
and carried away or to regain a unity
we all must have had sometime before

THE PATCHWORK PAVEMENT
OF THE LANE

tells a story of men who came with machines
to renew the surface over which unfeeling
automobiles glide, and a single manhole
alone provides a bump as a reminder

that below flows the effluent from
those who live and work not
in the lane (reserved for cars and
passers-through) but in offices and towers
whose backsides abut this back street

we climb down into the manhole
where history waits, and we can read
its layers or at least imagine them

once just dirt onto which rain fell and fell
washed away the paw prints of browsing
black bears, the jay dropping seeds
before Steller named it, before sails flapped
in the open water, unseen from here
before anyone called it a harbour, although

those who lived here long before clans of
mapmakers arrived, they drew up their canoes
in our prehistory (though not in theirs)
and had a name for all they saw, language
rich in salmon oil, blackberry, salal – but "lane"?

that word had to come later
when the need for a straight line between
two other straight lines laid itself
across landscape until then dense
with rainforest talking to itself
of the past that went back to
the land bridge gradually, glacially
awakening to Asia

I LOOK DOWN INTO
MY BACK LANE

mostly men without packages
not shopping, not on errands
they stop in a parking spot
cupping a hand against gusts
to light a smoke, stooped, they step
forward again, not with determination
not rambling either, the lane
not green or open or calm enough to warrant
pause or strolling – in caps and anoraks
legs thin and wide apart, so I can picture
skinny bodies under bulky sweaters,
and some unshaven ones can't remember
how to straighten their bones

would they like a word?
but what could I say? that if you look at
what keeps you unfree, that thing
most hard to look at
even if you can see it at all
much less name it, if, if ...

each man loyal to his own word
it might be defiance or dependence
difficult to deal with
though walking helps mightily

I could say, hey
you, down there, look up! (they never do)
it's not just me you'll see
yes, concrete balconies crowded
with flowering pots and higher still
the crows and gulls wheeling, and in time
if weather is willing, the unclouded moon
and her stars

ON THE DUAL NATURE
OF THINGS, I WRITE

that a solitary gull floats between high-rises
with aplomb and grace, gliding past
balconies far above my own
his immaculate white, airy curves
I may describe as angelic
that apparition-like way of arriving
then vanishing behind a tower
(saving his squawk for fellow gulls
or flapping, enraged crows)

yes, I know of his appetite and table manners
his strutting entitlement as he approaches
a burst garbage bag, his fury
when any other creature comes near
the blows his wings can deliver, the depth
his beak can sink into the soft stuff of the dead
his eagerness to eat what's vile
and leaking and staining asphalt
with a smear only winter rains will erase

but today he owns the air, he is beautifully
there, to remind me that his sea is near
and a joy to remember especially when
I recall my inland time in cities devoid of
sea-cries that prompt me here
to lift my eyes and watch his swift tilting
as he adjusts his trajectory to the flow
of wind blowing in from the west
from the ocean, which he helps me
celebrate: he says if I follow his flight
I will find that salty, sandy, flexible edge
along which I might stride, or stumble
if I am not aware of the flashing wave tips
offering their news of light to bird and man

THE YELLOW DOG HAS
NO APPREHENSION

about ice his master must negotiate –
his dog claws permit him to dance
under short-haired, pointy ears, to prance
off the lane into ornamental bushes
rife with messages from others
who also have been allowed the mercy
of a walk outside the condos where
they live, this perky one with a man
whom I deem an engineer

the way he extends the leash and then
pulls it back, untangling the pet who
never deigns to acknowledge his handler's
gesture, one of twirling the held tether
fingers twisting and refinding how to grip
to maintain control of animal urges
even as he himself feels the ice beneath
his brown dress shoes that shine so
I from up here can admire professionalism

and he does the wobble common to Canadians
of tipping off the slippery foot to balance
one arm raised, the body on alert in case
utter lack of movement is called for
in order to re-establish a proper connection
with Earth, simply assumed to be there
or else, like his furry friend, constantly
immersed in possibilities – and then they
pass safely on their way, neither as yet

weary of this journey into their city
with its winter sunshine and freedom
from walls, from the neighbour who insists
on music so loud, and even if eyes from all
those balconies are on him, he's like
Rusty, he cares only for the moment
that's new now and smelling fresh

THE SKINNY MAN
WITH THE STIFF LEG

kicks at a piece of trash
a white circle that once covered
takeout Thai food, and his good foot
is strong, the paper flies a little, achieves
lift-off before it settles to the edge
of the lane, marginalized

like the man himself, and I wonder
has he always taken a path where
he can walk and watch, directing
his discontent at rubbish – was it that
he loved and wanted love
that was not returned?

I've seen him standing where others
are hurrying, his baseball cap
down to hide his eyes
though his reddish hair sticks out

his freckled arms, his dusty pants
of the kind not seen anymore in stores
the lack of colour in his shirt
all tell me he is poor, that he wanders
the back street to keep himself company
to forget who might have propelled him
into some other way of being

he reminds us as we pass by
of our own faltering, as recent
as this morning when we thought of
someone who still matters
words, voice, text silent now
and the place we occupy
unfinished within ourselves
pushing forward, so we find
our centres lodged in other people
who have no knowledge
of our state, themselves busy with
moments of kicking garbage

SOME MEN ARE STRIDERS,
AND HERE'S ONE

lanky long legs clipping like scissors
along the lane, carrying two sagging bags
from Persia Foods as if they're weightless
it's too dark to see his demeanour
so movement carries the weight of impression
his upright strength overtakes and passes
other pedestrians: an encumbered woman
teenagers with their plugs and wires

he lopes as if he were on stage
confident as a man in his prime can be
with lines to deliver, words
that will cause heads to turn
to a moment of destiny arrived!
he is rehearsing that speech now
purposeful on his walk home

then a tow truck
with yellow lights casting ill shadows
forces him off centre, and he waits
on the verge taking in the truck's
slow prowl – and so minutes pass
legs braced apart, his head turned
I watch from here, he from there
the day is ending, we know there's little
left but to ponder whether it is nobler
in the mind to suffer unending self-regard
or be drawn in by the mundane, to see
which car might be towed, even if bags
still pull on both arms, cans of liquid
they must be or bottles, and there he stands
until the drama ends, the truck exits
at the far corner and disappears, unfulfilled

WHEN YOU DIED IT TOOK ME
MANY DAYS

before I stopped wondering each day
where you were, because you were
somewhere with all that fuel in you
for moving, never sitting still
a frequent comment your guests made
and as your brother I didn't hesitate
to agree, up and down you went
from outdoor table back to the kitchen
as we tried your new taste discovery:
oil, seeds, spice, perogies, chocolate

is it you in the lane with white hair
the upper back slightly bent, head
getting heavy from all it has thought?
is it the walk I identify? its mild
hesitancy, the pavement an opponent
requiring attention, tilt of the body
intensified in its forward thrust
almost a fall, a rehearsal for falling
and the cane in your right hand too far
out, more a tool for probing and
outreach than the balance you seek
when you achieve the elevator inside
that takes you up into the sunshine
of the lavish retirement tower

but even from here I can see she's
not you, you didn't have her money
not that it mattered in the end, and after all
the kidding about weather across town
your flatland fog, my mountainside cloud
now I sometimes miss thinking of you
for more than a day, and then you return:
my lane fills with mist after dark, the lights
ghostly, distance between them vast
no one out there you'd want to meet
except an old woman who would welcome
my note about this unusual atmospheric
veil and the moan of the harbour's horn
and I'd take her elbow and escort her
to the big door, see her through, watch
until she was finally gone home

reveals too little of the speaker
I take it to the balcony to be dispatched
because recycling is not sufficient
for its fate, and though I prefer
flame, I am matchless at the moment
and do not trust my oven where
I might thrust it headfirst
so its chill detachment will feel
a final, fatal heat reading its edges

I am waiting now, out here, folding
the page into a plane, its pointed nose
and aerodynamic wings perfect for launching
and still I wait, not for wind but for
the roar of the big red truck, its front lifters
ready to hoist the bin filled with our offal
and here it comes! vehicle stink and noise
permeating the lane, I look down into
what rumbles out of the bin into the opened
maw of the truck, and there I aim the poem

so truly it flies, so eagerly it joins the smell
that I have no doubt it recognizes
its rightful home, and with the next bin dumped
on top, what satisfaction it must feel
to join all that is unfit and taken away
never to be seen again

THE CROW LANDS,
INFUSED WITH PURPOSE

to explore a bag, perchance to find
the model morsel, the French fry
discarded or perhaps a crumb
of dignity in the doughnut not yet
mouldering, he steps close, closer
pecks and – behold! – is rewarded
his sunlit beak spies and digs and rips
he thinks neither ahead nor behind
tipping back to swallow the tidbit

I think of his feathers, black black, how
they absorb light, the dark hole
he brings wherever he lands on earth
always a purity of disappearance
his piece of night that darkens day
the underside of a shoe that waits
at the back of the closet whose doors
are locked, the key a child dropped
in the forest, moss swallowing it

and now Crow turns and the sun
flashes in his wings, a spark
and again the flash comes, lightning –
a sudden storming – to show me
that where black is, white will also be
if only briefly, yet briefly
suffices to make me look again
where I might have missed this
balance, his way of making light

as so many men lunge, his torso
tipped forward out of faded jeans
glasses blanking the world
so he sees only that step after step
won't allow inside emptiness
to suffice, to slow him
not into torpor but peace, peace
at least, at last, enough
so he can stop striding

his grey hair uncut in a while
arms swinging, but he's not noticeably
mad unless many are crazed this way
by the overflowing that drives us
into anonymous laneways
where we turn our faces away
to feel free from the scrutiny
and then disregard of others
– free of fleet entanglements –
no one to sidestep except one's self
which can't be done, there's no leaving
him behind, his hold reinforced
by every tread on this prowl

then the man is gone, out the end
of the lane – and has he felt the sunshine
that surely pulled him with its promise
from his rooms, and how is he now
when he turns the key and re-enters
the familiar where earlier he felt
stirring, then flooding, that urge
to plunge beyond silence?
how able to stand still instead
on the tiny atoll of mere continuance?

her hair long and black, and he
reaches up, pushes it back
to reveal her neck, which so
tempts him he leans in
and kisses her cheek as she
bends his way though neither
adjusts the pace of their movement

toward the steps of North Shore
Oncology – and no thought
about their public display (or
semi-public since only I see them
here in my eyrie watching for life)
not even a kiss of courage
to help with what waits ahead
this show of affection without
purpose except to enjoy lips
on beloved skin – given, received

the man hitches up his jeans
his wavy, stacked-up blond hair
his gait and gut all say his strength
remains, but his partner in navy
leggings walks also with a firm
step forward – and suddenly
they are neither patients nor
visitors but Adam and Eve with
their repertoire of innocent kisses
before fear was a word said by God

I TAKE THESE OLD PHOTOS
AND, DUMP THEM

off the balcony, friends I once knew
and loved, and love still though I
no longer think of them daily or even
weekly, have left their orbit
or they've misplaced me
among their own struggles
every day to keep from falling
into how we are when we are
ourselves without others

should I tear up this photo of Yvonne
before I fling it off? and this one of
one of the Toms? I let them fall as is
onto the cars parked below, whose roofs
they will rest upon until their owners
pick them off with puzzlement, look
momentarily but deeply into the eyes
of those faces, then drop them
onto the asphalt to disintegrate into mush

I return to my control room to think:
had I sent a rocket up, some message,
I might have found in myself
the courage to phone
seeking remembrance of times past
until we hung up with relief
and with anguish that we are
this way, so self-unanticipated
never noticing, as if our world had no moon
and no NASA to get anyone there anyway

INTO AIR SPACE ABOVE
THE LANE

pigeons dive, alight on roof rails
to begin their courtly dance, male
in metallic plumage, shiny armour
the white one shies away from

below the birds three tall girls
walk, holding hands, flouncing
pigtails and long legs, in that time
before they step out of homes

they reach the corner, still talking
easy teasing between girlfriends
boyfriends not seriously arrived
some boys always watching

I look up, the pigeons have flown
the lane turns from after school
to after work, more cars, these also
needing attention, the males here

speed but the blind corner slows
even the foolhardy, though not
among pigeons, who only consider
rules of the air that is everywhere

SHE'S DOWN THERE
EVERY DAY AT FOUR

ambling along the lane, on her cell
never hurried, always in jeans
with runners still white
and as she walks she leans
into the step she's taking
not seeing, focused instead
on the voice she's hearing

someone not here
not near enough to see, not anyone
she could walk to at her pace
that voice soothing, not saying
anything to make her stop
to frighten her with news
so that she drops the phone
in a moment remembered later
as the time she first heard that ...

the voice is asking about the evening
its chores ahead, the laundry
and calls that can't be put off
to register the children for soccer
to invite a colleague for dinner
unloading, loading the dishwasher
loving as best they can the mundane
aware that's where the desire
for a different life can lurk

and she turns back then, having reached
the end of her call, having gained
half the lane, a little distance along
in the day, and someone waiting

THE MAN IN THE LANE
TODAY, HAS HE

felt craving rise until he must walk
and then has he felt the longing dim?
a surprise to him who thought
his ache would connect him always
by its living urge to the world itself

he saunters now where others run, he sees
twigs on the trees others rush past
and he slows to watch pavement darken
with drops, at first only dottings, code
causing him to pull his collar up, surprised

he brought along the whole history
of desire but not his umbrella, and idly
he imagines some vector in the blood
that sounds Greek but ends in y
and cannot be cured though it can be

outlasted, a triumph that prompts
a gasp: to have lived years, years
to enter a later age when the soles
of his feet hurt, some directions
long discarded yet many steps remain

and now the lane ends in a T
he must decide which way to go
left, right, can it matter when either
takes him roundabout to where he began
to search inside solitude for what can be

found among its silences, sometimes
a little sound, as of a leaf falling or soon
budding open to its first wave of wind
so it revolves on a stem as if to see all
around the green that grows by the sun

I WISH TO ANNOUNCE
FROM MY BALCONY

to anyone who wishes to hear
that not far away lies a country
where the dead gather
they neither huddle nor grope
but unceasingly ascend – *expand?* –
beyond dimensions in space
the unending necessity of
understanding, now that time is done

ego has drained away with the blood
the hand finally stilled, its veins empty
rings shining nonetheless, remembering
gold and silver years now
nowhere except in the memory
of a few, until they forget almost
entirely, their own encumbrances
requiring more attention

here are the ashes we throw
into the sea, and here the photographs
we burn – but stamps from old postcards
we soak off: the 4-cent queen
glowing, cool, too young
for our flames
                        after we depart
the future still arrives to occupy
where we once stood knowing and
not knowing enough about either here
or hereafter or the voyage between
sudden as rupture or slow, enraptured

I WEAVE AN EFFIGY OUT
OF BLACK SOCKS

and pillow dust, a broken pencil
a torn shoelace for a smile
curl of pasta for a blind eye:
a disappointment, some one

I haul my creation to the balcony
and consider: give this thing
a sex and name? make it worthy
of the death I'm about to inflict?

but now children have gathered
below, their faces upturned in awe
to see a man wrestle with himself
in an unfamiliar, forbidden game

they wait, beyond anticipation
and I can see the boy at the back
would be first to open his arms
if I pushed this misery over

years later he tells his partner
a story of the day he almost caught
a man's shadow, so it seemed to him
a dark form, about to descend

but nothing came of it, the balcony
became ordinary again without
the shimmer of dream, the man
up there smiling down foolishly

shoving behind himself – what was it?
the children could never agree
though they each recognized
some thing needed hiding

I BESEECH ALL YOU
BELOW, PLEASE

work harder on your mouths
bring them into horizontal lines
less grim and discouraged
unnerved, unable to withstand
what the days have delivered
so smiles slide sideways and rot

I need only glimpse myself shaving
to know where I too belong
among those who have tried smiling
and produced rictus instead

left alone our minds don't care
how we look, so our mouths
reveal our constitutions and become
personalities of their own, some
gripped with snarl, threatening
to unleash the yellow teeth within
the fury of disappointments
pulling lips in different directions
but predominantly down, down
on both sides, eternally down, never
to be reconfigured in this life
set every day into scowls pressed
in flesh as if by a nasty upper hand

except perhaps one time looking up
at a clown in his mad pulpit
throwing down such exhortations
those walking below first think
police and then, relief arriving
with the blow of his harmlessness
landing, they feel the afternoon shift
with a sun returned to and lifting up

IN WINTER THE LANE
IS BLEAK, COLOURLESS

dominated by poles that carry silent
electricity, their top beams forming
crosses, these civic crucifixes marching
along and above without moving

four former trees that no longer sway
and even in the strongest winds
stay firm, bearing the weight
of wires where an occasional pigeon
rests though no bird nests here
ever, too exposed, too little purchase

do they notice when the light returns
when the air softens even if the rain
does not? surely they see how
the single alder begins its dance
this tree alone in the lane, gradually
sending out greenery to hide the
nakedness of the nearby pole
brushing it with the most tender
new-sprung leaves, and does the old
dried trunk forced into modernity
recall for that instant how it once
also lived, was green, aspired to
sun and cones and views
how it foresaw its natural demise
on the forest floor, a nurse log, not
this upright, unending rigidity
in the service of what cannot be
understood and was never imagined
in the time when the sap rose?

AT NIGHT DARKNESS
FILLS THE LANE

with a solidity unknown by day:
black flows in and obliterates
landmarks – what exists at noon
when seen by moonlight
glows inaccurately
all angles sinister

a rat races across the expanse
its eye providing a single spark
its claws on concrete a clatter so soft
it can only be heard in the hours
after midnight or after two on weekends
when residents succumb at last to sleep

occasionally a bulb burns above
this zone of collected obsidian and
stays alight throughout the night
to hold off fears, as if a face can fall
into its dreamtime shape more agreeably
while still illuminated, not loosening
as it might when dark steals from it
the strength of features known
at noon, what we know of one another

and wish to know, not wanting
that other creature whose slack jowls
and lips wet with drool turn us away
so we find ourselves looking out again
into the night and seeing in
windows the reflections we must
look beyond even if fearful that
what lies in the lane at this hour
cannot be good for us, the half
shapes that just a few hours ago
were bushes, poles, and posts
with no malign intent

I AWAKE IN THE MORNING
TO FIND

a large grey boulder has materialized
in the lane, where it blocks both cars
and pedestrians, its bulk so fierce
dogs draw back from their urge
to smell and mark, everyone
stunned by its presence, its way
of getting in the way, of saying
the unusual must be pondered
before progress can be achieved

soon the police arrive to flash
their blue lights on its flank
engineers measure its height
equal to the fifth floor of a tower
an irate civil servant pastes a warning
on its granite face, a child chips
at its surface with her toy hammer
a crow crosses above the mass
but decides not to descend

a local sage is called, and his slow
focus irritates those who want action
from this bent old beardless man
his musty backpack and silence
but as he communes with the stone
we see he has done this work before
I watch from my balcony: he sinks
his hand into the rock until
his arm vanishes up to the patched
elbow, then he bows his head and
his lips move in quiet incantation

later everyone tells the story
according to their own beliefs
scientific or esoteric, but all agree
he turned the stone into smoke
and by noon we were untroubled
once more, though I for one
wish I had rushed down to taste
the earthy essence of the mineral thing
before the mystery left us
with nothing but ourselves again

and the air fills with liquid falling
coolly from clouds unable to lift
themselves over the mountain
that rises up the street? those
strutting, cooing aerialists who
seem always to flutter and twirl
along rails and roofs are absent then
as if the torrent swept them away
into bubbling gutters along with
their droppings and feathers

I understand they, too, are complex
creations even if my perch above
the lane provides a view of them
as beings interested only in food,
flying, procreation, none of which
earns more than a cursory bobbing
of my head, convinced as I am
that other matters of consciousness
impossible to articulate in single nouns
are more worthy of the effort needed
in flights of imaginative thought

on days when the rain does not stop
even then sometimes I hear that
distinct flap-flap their wings make
as they launch themselves onward
occasionally upward so that one
may alight on wires near my window
and peer in, not to judge but to see
that inside creature's stillness
not unlike its own when it rains

AT LAST I SEE THE MAN
I'M WAITING FOR

walking in the lane, his gait distinct
the manner of bending his knees an
utter ease in the strength of his prime
what he's wearing not significant
jeans, jerseys that are everywhere
unlike his walk, his way of moving
his body forward through space his
and his alone, without thinking so

I am waiting for him as I wait for
anyone below who calls my attention
by voice, by shoes or carry bag or
hairdo, or how they manage rain
the little dogs, the bouncers yapping
the strollers and the smokers, those
who glance, those who stare nowhere
those with canes, walkers, high heels
children darting away from the group

I am waiting for the man to go on
into his life, not as if I could stop him
what would my yelling do except
stall his steps briefly, and after all
letting him go is good practice for
those others who have walked into
my life and then walked out, we all
have them, those beautiful ones we
once could not imagine being without

THOSE I HAVE SAID
GOODBYE TO

have not left, they stay
and haunt me – not just
the dead but those too alive
to turn my way – and I ask
can I learn this skill

to live utterly on my own
not wishing or needing
from anyone what's missing
in my own skin with its flaws
that I can forget when among

others? though not just *any* others
not the idlers in the lane
with whom I've shared no
afternoon coffee and consolation
but rather the ones I've recognized

even if already some of those
have excarnated into dross
and angel fare – and the living
have stopped stopping by
bound by their own futures –

so is this my choice then?
to go into the evening light
and breathe it all the way
inside as an ally I can rely on
to say yes, or to dally

and wait for myself to grasp
that, like reluctant millions
before me, I'm learning to die
by seeking always to live
as nightfalling air turns cold

AS THIS MAN WALKS
HE TILTS, FAVOURS

his right hip so the left foot swings
slightly outward and defines his
orbit, bound by rules he hasn't made,
accommodation required by tiny

bones in his foot, larger in the leg
blue denim neatly pressed because
he's of that age, balding fellow
with the laurel fringe of curly white

pulls from his pocket a cloth
also white and stabs at his nose
stuffs the rag back in his jeans
lifts a shoulder, turns his head left

as if to see for that moment all
of a once-possible life, his throat
extended, the ropy muscles alert
for a tableau next to the parking garage

for a picnic table, baskets, blankets, waves
a dozen children leap on sloping sand
fathers and mothers look up warmly
from their kicking, pin-diapered babies

for him settling down with a beer
leaning back, tatty paperback bent
on his chest, closed eyelids under sun
bright red, eyes that love all this goodness

no death in sight, none just passed that
shook them, not even the thought
as a hand lifts his book to read
how far he had reached before sleep

I STEP OUT FOR AIR
BUT IT IS NOT

air that greets me – a sunbeam
bounces from a tower window
slants off my eyeball
vibrates, splinters and declares
it flies without jest, reflected
from afar, pure colourless
cold fire yet as near as blood

so the joke's on me, those
winking, jangling waves
catch my brain off guard
when it's muddy and grave
obsessed with its own heavy
workings, and this light intends
to evoke the buried dance

not stabbing my retina though
it might have, not blinding me
though it might have, but spinning
its story of distance travelled
through night populated by
objects huge and suspended –
always leaving, always arriving –

merely to materialize here with
an unflashy message not unlike
my own, because standing here
on my balcony I've also arrived
haven't I? come from somewhere –
the kitchen just now, before that
the womb – so I have journeyed

always turning to meet the one
whose blaze flared and found
me, went into and beyond
soundlessly, unstoppable, though
the moment I beheld it, didn't it
also hold itself in me, wanting to
rest awhile in a warm dark home?

HOW EASILY I CHANGE

into the person I am
growing toward, he's already
in our common future
and to reach him I need
do nothing (and to hurry
only smudges my path)

at night, in bed, I feel he comes closer
as near as the lane, managing its dark
tapping along, not stumbling
where two pavements converge
into a lip – he needs no light, generating
his own though no one
can see his glow, except I see it

the unencumbered one
who waits for me
willing to take from me
what I willingly give –
in no other way can I pass to him
the weights that are mine
that are also his –

one night, we unite
and go somewhere – not here –
mist from the inlet
as it rises up
and alerts the foghorn
to begin mourning

AS THE RAIN FALLS,
DISTANCE INCREASES

between those who walk in the lane –
a blue curtain settles on each face
in a nearly impenetrable veil
that holds back thoughts from flying
outside their originator and soon
they degenerate into gloom

what's needed is the sun of another mind
a glance that doesn't immediately turn away
but stays an extra second to acknowledge
being seen is important in breaking out of
the fortress bubble of one's own self

a child will provide such a chance
the way he prances from puddle to puddle
his yellow raincoat an assertion, his mother's
umbrella pointing upward though she
focuses on her child and on the grey street
where she seeks not for the pennies
she once found but for the thought she had
on the day of his birth, a sunny day
when all the air was light

and she basked in wishes from so many
some far away in places seldom
deranged by downpour though dust
and snow can also cast a pall that
causes the soul to shrink if the mind
is impoverished in seeing how (here
for example) rain spills its language
on our earth, spelling nothing
except the words we raise there

comes when rays of setting sun
extend their promise out of
the sky and provide to earth
filmic beams, reminding us
biblical times are here, too
even if a holy hour lasts visually
only one minute as light strikes
up through clouds into space
we believe was made for us

but here in the lane we cannot see
this brief beauty: our apartments
block the way west, and yet
we gain in what is reflected above
on high windows: a surging
glow deepens and presents orange
rectangles behind which we know
families gather for meals, some
squabbling, pulling down blinds
not wanting the blinding final
glare gifted to them in the turning
from one time of day to another

older loners look and ponder
who they are to have arrived here
in this fading, the clouds a painting
of a master colourist in gold and grey
and cream and beige and a blue that dims
its cerulean in honour of coming night
to become as transparent as a page
I might write upon had I a stylus
of lightning or a wand built from
the brightness of an evening star

I FEEL THE LAMENT
IN ME GROWING

I want to cry out about people
seasons that have passed
natural phases in one way
yet the part of my spirit that aches
aches every day and never tires
… except just now I'm claimed

by a man carrying bags homeward
plastic pulling on both hands
his wife with the small dog
turns walks into twirls
to untangle the leash while he
puts his feet down again and again

tomorrow I will salt my clouds
with joydrops, so these people will
turn to one another for longer
than before, and when the man sets
the bulging white bags on the table
it's no more than a sigh that she hears

READING ABOUT
AN OLD MAN DYING

I look to the lane for balance:
one man wears a gold chain
one in sandals, both slow
of step, conversing, smiles
exchanged, no thoughts
of the kind I am thinking

these heavy men unfit
for running (the sandal
flapping, likewise the chain)
have not finished their course
each draws the other on
into plain convivial day

but at night if they lie awake
what consolation would each
muster, from where, and could
reading the written thoughts
of another man serve
in the place of prayer?

on how to open wet, clammy umbrellas
the splatter factor that must be considered
so those nearby fall out of range
of flying drops before the *flump* that
indicates success in unfurling

and even so I see in the lane
those who prefer to walk in drizzle
to keep their hands free in case
a friend from the far past appears
and requires hand shaking or whole-
body hugging, difficult if a wet thing
dangles between them, or a dog
suddenly crazed by some smell
in their clothes leaps forward
into the punch delivered betwixt
its eyes with a dexterous free right hand

and the boys in the lane soon learn
to handle umbrellas like swords
thrusting them at one another, placing
their feet just so, yelling "en garde"
while their mothers swat at them with
purses, admonishing their young
to be more genteel yet secretly admiring
their panache, remembering the fathers
of these children had once been gallant
(before they came home harried by work)
in that sunny time when love grew daily
and rain meant they could dream
under its drumming without thinking
of the stuff to carry out of the house
each morning: keys, lunch boxes, phones
though no one thought "umbrella" until
out of nowhere came the rain

SO MUCH TIME
IS SPENT WAITING

for whatever comes next: recess or break
a birthday or Christmas, for a mechanic
to fix the flat, for a woman to leave
for a man to come, child to speak up
for ringing in the head to stop
a flight to arrive, for lab results
the chance to start over –
                                              but
the middle-aged smokers in the lane
have shared a joint after visiting
one of their mothers in the retirement home
and now, grinning, duty done, neither
holds out for a future, the woman
leaning on the man in the laughing present

until they arrive at home where
minor responsibilities assert themselves:
who will make tea? one will while one waits
and soon they are silent, settling in
where memories replay and cluster
to remind them the elder they saw
is already waiting for their return

and waiting not for her supper
or evening's piano playing or TV shows
but for pictures that arise from her past
when she was hard-pressed by offspring
yet anticipating their silence in bed at last
free to enter the night world
of her own making, without delay

I TAKE OFF MY GLASSES
AND THE LANE BECOMES

a blurred rainy Paris as my floaters
drift over the lights and obscure
momentarily any bright intent, then
someone shouts "garçon" for more
vin de table and the dignified ladies
and old gentlemen smoke Gitanes
and no one notices the poodle defecating
in the manicured park except perhaps
the solitary who steps in merde

I put my glasses back on to fathom
better where I have been, understanding
that it is not so easy to leave the earth
where I live even were I wanting
to become temporarily parisien

outside the poles have not changed
into Belle Époque streetlamps, and no
bridge covers a famous river, nothing
is noteworthy, no brochures wax
ecstatic about this view, no one takes
a selfie with this background, everyone's
on the way elsewhere, not even bothering
to think the place a disappointment

except sometimes I think this way, think
hard about how I came here and not
to some other, more beautiful, famous
place, knowing some would consider
I'd failed somehow, though nonetheless
at night when the traffic eases, I can sleep
and my dreams are substance enough
so in the morning I awake to fresh air
and (a short walk away) croissants
though the English muffins taste better

HOW MANY OF US
REMAIN UNFINISHED

I wonder when I look down to the lane
and see someone I cannot fully see
half-hidden under his umbrella
wind occasionally lifts to reveal
moustache and frown, swarthy
sunken cheeks so perhaps a foreigner –
aren't we all, as we lean against
rain and without saying as much
ask how do we access the good god
part of ourselves that often arrives
only as a curse, not what we crave
although what that man below wants
I cannot know – only the highly attuned
among us can pick up all frequencies –
I sense nothing at this distance
except haste in the way he shifts
the umbrella to his left hand
without a glove, a black umbrella
but even so how easy to picture
part of him collapsing when the one
he wants does not want him, a state
that completes incompleteness and that
he works at denying, knowing eventually
all desire dims like a shoreline
when the ship sails, and on its deck
he tastes salt wind alone

IF ONLY I COULD TAKE PICTURES
WITH MY EYES

the photographer said, if I could capture
what I see without the bother of Nikon
I would satisfy daily that eternal need
to create beauty brought forth by light

I remember her words this winter day
the lane below filling with darkness
as it rises first to windows to peer in
its long grey arm reaching the wall switch

that brings light to the table where I sit
flowers nearby, necessary participants
in the fading afternoon, telling stories
of spring and bloom, speaking only of

applying colour now against night
never once sending me back into
a time where I ... what does it matter?
their fragrance still without decay

I WAS TIRED OF LIVING ALONE,
SHE SAYS

and with the bundle she clutches
she contrives to sidestep loneliness
for years – decades – by then
she'll outstrip the need for others –
and kisses the baby's head as it
bounces against her breast –
this chattering with a friend
savours present and future both

they pass out of sight below
leave me alone with my thoughts
about the quandary of yearning
and the question of the father
a passerby in a pub night
and is *he* floundering or
crowded by mute feelings
now he is once more
forlorn, his bed a familiar only
to his own dark labours?

I return to the child I believe
is a boy, one version of his story
streaming into him with mother's milk
as he grows onward past pablum
and toward the iron of meat
his little teeth strong, and he himself
ready to revise any notion not his own

DOGGONE IT,
IS THERE ANYONE DOWN THERE

whose loyal and communicative dachshund
died early like a Romantic poet, convulsing
on the bed, bulging eyes straining to see
how the coming elsewhere stains the sheet?

or who believes that a stone carried
can carry one across a stretch of silence
onto that grassy plain where dogs run happy
but never defecate, freeing only their limbs?

or who's haunted by a name consecutively
given to different dun-coloured spaniels, each
with problem ears wherein lurk bacteria
the same vet cleans, intoning "Lucy, Lucy"?

or who suspects he was once a rescue dog
ultimately untrainable, always barking
always returned and kept behind wire
on the lookout for unattainable times?

or who like me chews on a stick and drops it
hoping someone will pick it up again, chews
on a phrase and cracks it, finds a new shtick
in furious need, frothing and half-sick?

he bends to write on the lane's
pavement with a child's chalk
without others? and expecting
an adult's answer, a reply
in capitals, he leaves the white
weightless chunk and waits, considers
the predicament of anyone who lives
alone, children up and flown with
kindred of their own kicking
on a change table in naked delight
or saying a-b-c and then something
more, words flavouring, dismaying

so, no one to talk him through thoughts
discarded when seen in a social
light, the glow from others
reminding him what he cannot produce
on his own: the quick uplift of laughter
at the childish scrawl on the street
the white words already blurring
under trampling feet, in the rain
its plea dissolving down dark drains
where a congregation of rats
unable to comprehend its code
turn to one another while up above
anyone eager to find messages
might be advised to look elsewhere
in the world, upward

HOW I WOULD LIKE
TO SEE A SHIP

in this laneway, a foreigner
with canvas flashing full of wind
All Sails Set, my school reader
dropped decades ago, the tattered
spine fading, an occasional coloured
illustration slipping out, intent
on escape from words, black vines
crawling page after page full of rhyme
and meteors here and there falling from
stars, characters unlike the reader
with his constant calling to the absent

oh, how he wants to be startled into
his former self, the child who never
saw the sea for years, years
but always knew it would be there
when he needed it, the song of
its shore repeating and telling him
to watch and listen and to imagine
what might lie ahead in the firmament
yes, even here amid towers
with only rain willing to speak
of journeys still to come in a time
when he'd become an old salt
eager for bed and the day safely done
the sun down yet set to begin again

NO BORDERS RUN THE LENGTH
OF THE LANE

it's easy to cross from either side
if a delivery truck takes up the width
no guard stands there, nodding us
forward, his hand open to receive
documents, gun on his hip, supreme
clarity in his eye, an upright protector
younger than my children, so I have
the answer he wants when he asks
about my plans for his country: visiting
family, and I am stamped, passed
and a little unnerved to be seen
so without threat when I feel in myself
various upheavals readying

nothing so worrisome here, nothing
severe, though still it happens that we
cross from one of our selves to another
sometimes a simple drop almost
unnoticed, not the way we register
the lane in our shoes that need
new soles to soften the patchwork
around the drain, the grey hardness
where we stumble onto understanding
how we are divided from others, that
truck driver who swings out of his cab
plunks his baseball cap on backwards
and pulls on bent leather gloves
ready for unloading, a being in boots
landed among us and whom we admire
here outside the retirement high-rise
a country with one exit only, though he
alone notes the stacked boxes
of frozen peas, fish sticks, prunes

I'D LIKE TO CHECK OFF

engaged and *content*
to indulge the urge
for fullness, not stuffed
as in sick, but always present
plus reaching (and careful
with the raw times
that come from inside and
out: events, loved ones)

I can resort to comparison
to The Voice known on the street
his timbre distinct, deep, as if drunk
but he's not, and with flourish
in his arms and legs he speeds
on his way, a lanky man

so it's on to reaching: just that
by imagining others ... gathering
with their backpacks and bandanas
but who can say? all I can say
it's better to take notice:
the way smokers dispose
of their butts, how the terrier
pulls the master, the honking
at crosswalks, a shout, so sudden
the erasure of the unseen day

from those walking below
how I want just one more juicy meeting
of merry limbs and the dog on the leash
held by the woman a bit bowed by
years of desire turns to his mistress
surprised by a new perfumy vibration
then returns to messages left in grass

if only I had tried a little harder back then
comes floating up often in the afternoon
wafting by in a dark balloon, almost black
air seeping out of its wrinkled self
impossible to continue up to heaven for
those answers, sinking back to the thinker

I like it here but it's not like home
in this city of immigrants, skin tone
and body shape common, comfortable
still the yearning carries on, causes
feet to drag, the overheavy briefcase
no substitute for lively, dancing nights

and it's true, the clarity of
our last incarnation will be as birds
causes the gulls to scream and
the crows to somersault down from
perches, starlings chatter
their secret has been revealed

I RECOGNIZE THOSE WHO
HAVE WRITTEN

in the book of grief, over and over
the names scrawled in black ink
on the one page each of us is given
to record those who have left

this thin man below, his newspaper
folded, a club he beats against his leg
hand hooked in a box of beer
its cardboard colours festive

declaring a social evening at home
with chips and slaps on the knee
guffaws with a friend, though always
he walks here stiffly, teetering, alone

I open the balcony door, step into rain
with its cool, unchanging touch
that falls on my face, soft fingers
to pull from me, to wash from me
salt grime after someone close has died

I see her love of flowers everywhere
when I walk, she comes to mind
where the rhododendrons bloom
the smell of earth made richer
by a shower eager in its slanting

I LOOK STRAIGHT OUT,
NOT DOWN:

a robust grey male pigeon
balances on a white female
who herself steadies on the round
railing of the rooftop opposite
while the cock's wings flap
above their heads some seconds
performing high-stakes acrobatics
I saw him earlier strutting
sideways on the rail, his breast
puffed, but the hen sidled away

and now he is delivered into
their cloacal kiss, all his displaying
ended, and she meeting him
as counterpart, no penetration, just
union and equilibrium both

those below miss this creative act
occupied by their own requirements:
to escape others, to find others, to live with
or even become others, to get out from under
the weight of others, of parental stories
and of the sound of the talking self
to want to hatch out and launch
into imagining no obstacles
in the air ahead, how buoyancy is all
balance as simple as tilting a wing

BENT MAN BELOW,
YOU MAY HAVE HEARD

yourself mumble while you walk
and sometimes stumble on your ever-
returning regrets over deeds done
people turned away, indifferent
but still no scarlet R emerging
on your chest, its ridges
each year more vivid than
a birthmark even if both you
below and I above see the signs
in ourselves and in those nearby:
lines weight the mouth at forgotten
corners where truth gathers its glue

but now look up, I say to that man
who bends beneath the satchel of thought
he hoists each morning: see the evening
bird: Flicker lands atop the tilting
power pole, looks right and left
shows his bright throat patch to sun
dips back, tips forward, dives into
air, a swimmer riding a swoop down
wings open only enough to break
his descent to the nest where work waits
and mastery and the family bustle
and if this is not sufficient to refresh
and reset a default, does he not
remind us the next step can be
revived, if not by thought then at least
by gliding away to dream, the pillow
safe, the sheet drawn up but not over

I WATCH THOSE
WHO ARE STRONG

and admire how easily they continue
with worrying about tasks assigned
and self-assigned, not just the day's
checklist but that greater endeavour
of purpose amid chaos and decline

and when the cup can no longer
be lifted, the lips chapped, unable
to accept the proffered cool water
will these souls reclaim a former
strength, gaining not muscle but

the manner of looking beyond?
as they do here walking in the lane
minds filling with work and more:
the love they give and also receive
the rainy air kissing their cheeks

while a smile from a passerby who
expects no return gift lets them grasp
that today it's best when we look
outside ourselves to find the offerings
bestowed, ready-made for our eyes

ABOVE THE LANE
THE CLOUDS BREAK APART

as indifferent to themselves as to us
though their grey and white patterns
suggest playfulness or at least ease
with self-destruction, not the case
with those who stamp the pavement
to hold off November by movement

the sunlit fringes of cumulus race
ahead of the slow mother cloud as if
they're heralds of joyfulness ready to
announce to the blue sky that horizons
must be reached whenever the wind
stretches invisible fingers eastward

I ponder our vast differences
clouds and us, and also between
us below, so much cannot be said
yet glimpses do occur, fleeting wisps
at ground level, winter breaths
exhaled as ghosts of our former selves

A TALE OF TWO
NEIGHBOURS BEGINS

when the man in the apartment below
hears me coughing and must wonder
what I have done to produce this
often hollow yet thick sound of
someone slowly making his way
beyond himself, he must certainly
want me to improve my health
so he can lie abed without above him
this reminder of human frailty
or perhaps he's grown accustomed
to my rattling as we both no longer hear
the trucks and drunks outside our balconies
who pass by in their business while we
imagine what we might have become
had we lived less alone, had there been
a loved one to administer balm
some lozenge of hope that we might
yet be wrong about the future

waiting with its silence – oh yes
he's a decent man who now and then
plays his music in the dark
warmly accompanied by scotch
so he forgets I'm lying awake
with the reverb coming up through
my pillow, and it's not that his choice
of tunes offends, mostly instrumental
thankfully no vocals added to the mix
except it does wake me up when I wish
instead to stay in that quietness
that dreams provide even when
everyone there is talking at once
a disturbance I sometimes carry
into daylight, mine arriving earlier
than his, I don't actually tiptoe at dawn
and I suspect grinding my coffee
enters his slumber, calls him
to attend to the things ahead
he put off last night in favour of
the comfort of lonely songs

THE CROW FLIES IN,
LANDS ON A POWER LINE

does not waste time considering us
except as garbage makers who toss
half a Tim Hortons in the gutter, morsel
as banquet, though the crow knows
not to quarrel with the big gull
whose high stepping does not waver
in assault, outsized beak open
approaching angel-white wings
raised, ready for blows

I caught a crow one day looking in
from the railing, head cocked
better to see geraniums, bananas
in a blue bowl on the table
and me sitting, one hand holding
a book that wanted to close, its spine
so new – and what did he think?

it's hard to imagine what I
would say were I to see myself
for the first time this way: of a certain age
the individual harder to pinpoint
but what he might see before
he flips his black judge's robes
and steps into air and away
his snake eye on the hunt for what
can be eaten without hands
I think it's better not to say

HERE COMES A FACE
MADE UGLY

by male anger, the twist of mouth
barely holding back curses
and the muttering ready to blow
as his lips protrude, ears glow red
eyes hooded yet unable to contain
the hurt self, and these combine
to frighten one who might bring
solace, if there even *were* anyone
whose presence softened his visage
and what could I do to draw him
from the bile that rises, and recalling
what works for me, I yell down
"Look up and let it rain in your eye"

but he does not hear, he's stepped
so deeply alone into himself that
he cannot be reached, and I hesitate
to fling anything else his way – surely
if words fail, my rose petals would
drift past unnoticed, my small
poems shaped into paper darts
would strike against his cap, a further
irritant against which he would rage
to be so bothered by the world when
all he wants is to be free from it

whereas today I love all I survey
with such surety that I may step
from this perch – the air half supports
my falling self, and as I speed toward
this maddened one, he will blurt out
in astonishment all that plagues him
so my landing, hard as it is, makes
him fumble with his phone
and shock softens, reverses
what a moment ago he loathed

BEST ANSWER FOR HOW TO REVIEW
YOUR MISTAKES

take them for a walk, stride for stride
they fall behind, your shadow
thinning, you can feel more light

but it's only the *lane* you must see
not the future that you fill with
scenes of what might happen *if* ...

so avoid that slip, it's essential
to make both past and future cease:
you're at the busy part of the lane

cars turning thoughtfully into retirement
home parking, men dead set for the Legion
the librarian smokes and strolls

dawdles, never not on his phone
and no urgency, more a continuing
of a thread to one person equally there

A BODY FALLS OUT
OF THE SKY, LEGS UP

the heavy head dropping first, this
I fear from the towers that rise
above the lane where I watch
unidentifiable ... women? men? seldom
children? scurrying on high balconies
press against railings, lean far out
not suspecting the sudden give
of rain-soddened support until
someone tumbles, arcs, grasping air

I stand rooted on my ledge, shooing
pigeons away, tend to geraniums
scissors in hand, snipping deadheads
always aware of the edge as close
as choice itself, though certain annihilation
might turn into broken only, unable and
immobile and a brain babbling
that the angel one hoped for did not
materialize, instead now shrill voices
of *should have* and *never ever, never ever*
and *never ever again* on the ward
all windows closed against any
fluttering beyond the pane

WHEN THE FACE
OF SORROW APPEARS

in the lane below, I feel pity
start up in me, how sadness marks
an old face, that man whose wife
stepped off their common path
to become spirit, and I cannot speak
about her new world except to say
leaving this one has creased his

so now his mouth curves down
into a sickle that cuts his flesh off
from others who long to hold him
back from his own torment even
as they know their reaching out
creates only one moment of ease
among the hours of questions
that circle by day and then collect
at night on his pillow to write
the same story he reads each dawn

unsteady in his walk, careless
in his dress, two days unshaven –
anyone can look this way now
and then, not notice what others
notice, not care about niceties –
these can be managed, but his face
cannot be altered or tidied up
it lives its own life and will not
yield to what the mind says in
platitudes, not one able to loosen
the grief each day choking him

until eventually ... I think it is
too soon to speak of acceptance
though surely a morning will alight
on his brow when he will take up
her favourite coffee cup and not be
beset by the past, when and where
they bought it, but instead
re-enter love before pain and
linger there, his hand curving
to hold the handle she once held

DEAR CITY FATHERS
OR MOTHERS OR PLANNERS

please build a European fountain
in my back lane, to bring a springing
ivory foam continuously spurting
and dropping on stones that grow
wet black moss thick as otter fur –
and please, only stones, no mounted
archduke trumpeting his triumph over
us commoners below, his history not
transportable: here we acknowledge
lineage only of earth and its upheavals

and I do so admire white water
shooting high *and* falling as if to remind us
down is as natural as up and that all energy
returns to earth, the sound of persistent
splashing renews me now, and I swear
I'll be the most ardent listener, learning
day after day to detect the cadence
each bubble bursting makes as it
crashes on rock and delights children
clustered below, their nervous mothers
bent and hovering, unaware of wheeling
pigeons that drank their fill and then
startled themselves into up-flapping and
following into air their one white leader
above a single civic worker who sweeps
trash and keeps clean our attraction to
uplifting water music so unlike the rain
falling now with its measured drumming

for surely they are among us, mystified
by the ease with which we ignore
their pleas, their hands reaching for us
and gaining no purchase on our anoraks
or by children who run pell-mell
through their beseeching and hear
none of their cries, nothing to quiet
a boy's shouts of ready-or-not

at the opening to the high-rise garage
an old wraith waits every day
blessing families who roll out
by touching her hand to the roofs
of the cars that pass oblivious
to her checklist and to her desire
that the newborns at least be safe
in a world that took from her
the warm and pulsing blood
she never thought of much until
it left and she became this other
creature of longing, standing
at the clanging mechanical gate just as
farther along another from
her realm causes the dogs to shiver
and snarl at nothing, or so it seems
to their owners, who pull at leashes
and worry their pets are ailing
crazed by forces no vet can locate

if the veil were lifted from our eyes
would we see such a mass of spectres
we could never again descend
to the street, our lungs fearful
of drawing in air filled with
the desire of phantoms not to leave us
to once more walk through time
as if existence were only now
and not forever?

I WENT TO THE DOCTOR
AND THE DOCTOR SAID

ten years, twenty, one week
or thirty minutes to walk home
step onto my balcony once more
craving the return of my old
life – why didn't I love it
better, respect and cherish
the way it was at ease with time
never thinking too far ahead
even if I can't deny those days
of fussing over trivial details
and fruitless melancholic fretting

I look over the precarious railing
try to imagine who below might
carry a known deadline, but no one
can guess correctly, not the child
leaping foot to foot, her father
nearby, checking his phone
neither tired of the day, each
in a circle that overlaps and joins
their lives together, not just today
but for years even if one of them
has an appointment waiting

so an hour passes, then a year
then ten, and a slow procession
winds toward the sea, and as
I am carried along, I look up
to see someone new on my
former balcony – a young man
looks down at me and those
following, more curious
than moved, already backing
into his kitchen, preparing
for guests he expects will fill
an evening with laughter erupting
from their never-ending futures
and no mention of any procedures
or weary nurses cleaning up

THAT BLACK THING
ON THE PAVEMENT

isn't moving, and from this distance
I think first of Cranberry
the cat, and his story, given to a child
as a companion, outgrown by the child
naturally, decades ago
so whatever is down there
lying on the pavement is not
what my imagination throws up

I wait awhile, observe further
strain my eyes to find
definition but against grey concrete
the thing looks like a black hole
through which I might enter
the underground, not just of
stones and packed earth
a million times packed
by cars, trucks, feet, strollers

but a light-filled tunnel, stairs
that lead down, then level off
with occasional pools reflecting
torches in walls growing higher
until the ceiling recedes entirely
and above me … stars
but in daylight, perfectly seen
Milky Way and sun equally ablaze

this the kind of lift I feel
because along comes a kid
early teens and gawky though I can see
he'll be handsome, and he kicks
the black thing, and it lifts easily:
a dropped rag a workman
left behind, he of a small coterie
the disguised among us
who know what dark cloths can bring

see the impressions my wet toes make
on the fresh-washed bathmat? it needn't
get any more personal than that
I won't talk about my struggle with whatever
and you will not be expected to exclaim
about the view down into the lane
though the perspective will honestly
surprise you, you might make one true
sound when you look out and see
how unseen you can remain

maybe you'll see the redhead
go by, how once on her man's arm
she flicked her hair, looked back and up
caught me: my attentive beam
on her comely nape had drilled in
but you wouldn't see her eyes
she never looked up again and though
tempted, you could tell, her pride
carried her forward until safely
past, self-conscious country behind her

I won't ask you to comment on
drivers or how their cars take on character
as they age, colours stuck in time and
simultaneously fading, I wouldn't want
to suggest even by the way I speak softly
that parallels exist between automobiles
and us, there is no us, of course
and right now I see it's not
more talking we need, it's quiet
we both crave more than company
so thanks anyway for coming by

a hundred eyes look down
and spot me on my balcony!
usually no one looks, one perch
here, another there, with flowers
or without, furniture undergoing
transformation by rain into
mould, scum darkening wood

but on the full moon it could happen
every tenant in the tower on
its north and west sides peers up
each at the same time only
to find the moon obscured
cloud cover at its natural best
and yet they've been drawn there
the moon has its reasons

and they turn as one mind
so many pressed against windows
leaning over railings, settling for
a neighbour not observed till then
who seems not to notice any of them
though now, wait, he looks up

HE WHO HESITATES
IS LOST IS NOT

what the squirrel down there
is thinking, his black tail long
as his body, twitching, his head
twisting, claws gripping pavement
certain something automotive
his way comes – but he can see
nothing – and who has not failed
in one of these ways: stalling
when we should have run or
blindsided when we thought the sea
in sight, the beach umbrella
eager to open over our sleepy selves

dear black fellow, today is not
your end-day – for the Mercedes
rolling into the retirement home
is not in any hurry for your death
which it wishes neither to cause
nor to see, so it slows while you
freeze in panic and indecision both –
then with a bound toward the edge
you excite yourself by once more
evading the fate you've heard of
on the way to nutty trees impossible

to live without, their shade and
sweetness offered freely, and in
a moment between chatter and dash
between climbing and leaping
it comes to you, this blood-thought
that just as the sun passes overhead
so too the summer heat is waning
even as you pause there among
the leaves green with juice

TODAY I HAVE DISCOVERED
AGAIN HOW

to lie on my couch and listen: out there
cars pass by, slowly or determined
to arrive first wherever their destination
the drivers secondary, only there
to make booming music ripple out and
greet all no matter their need for peace
which comes but not always when called
seldom when needed, oh, if only
my legs, so distant from my heart
not moving the length of the couch
could turn themselves to ears, ha, to catch
the quiet always fleeing and always ending
at a soft place like these pillows, soundless

I listen, and as the noises dim to only
a Sunday's occasional beep, I hear
what has been patient and now has
stepped forward, with a voice familiar
yet more than my own talking
more like my father's when he explained
in his toolshed the alchemy of fire
and steam and tongs, his eye
on his son to see if he understood, more
like my mother's when she shelled peas
on the steps, mosquitoes not yet launched
from their secret leaves, every ear attuned
to her words, even more to the humming
of the hymn that helped her live

SUDDENLY THE HEART EASES,
I DON'T KNOW WHY

what has changed? winter light gives way
and night replaces day, I draw the curtains
pause to see (without seeing) the lane
fill, empty, fill again slowly, slowly empty
no dramatic collision, no yelling, all
urgency elsewhere, here is only me

who feels relief, for whatever gnawed
gnaws no more, my fretting's source
this time a friend, but it might have been
a piece of news arriving by midnight
phone, or that wing that brushed
my face as I was born, how it wanted me

to chase its source, to live haunted
by its memory, that I might seek and seek
and be rewarded – once and then later maybe
once more – by the lifting of weight, unconnected
to the dying glow off cars nosing the lane,
still, the softening of their metal does ignite

a measure of gratitude for the way life is
passing: am I not upheld now and then?
and brought to the front of myself so
I can say, I am here, I will continue
let the tumult contain me for soon
soon, it will become my time to fly

OF COURSE THE GODS
HAVE FLED THE LANE

filled it with film trucks, attendants
while I want skylarks to ascend
and remind me I have a destiny
waiting, if not here then beyond
men and women bedecked
with tools at their waists, phones
in their hands, duct tape dangling
all creating light and shadow
to entertain us when we get glum
because we're ordinary after all

yet ordinary is so vast it's enough
or should be even if not complete
that god part missing, replaced
even if irreplaceable – still, we're
good at adapting to lesser forms

that the crow that lurks at the edge
of this stuck cavalcade doesn't sing
as sweetly as the storied lark
doesn't limit his intelligence, and so
I urge my thinking to accept
the day as is and what it offers me
which might not be the highest light
but still the sun lands on the dark bird
and makes it shine

ACKNOWLEDGMENTS

Special thanks to those who read or heard various versions: Robert Adams, Nicola Goshulak, gillian harding-russell, Lorna McCallum, Meg Stainsby, Richard Therrien, Russell Thornton.

"in winter the lane is bleak, colourless" was published in *Worth More Standing*, an anthology of tree poems edited by Christine Lowther and published by Caitlin Press in 2022.

"the patchwork pavement of the lane" was published by *Windfall*, a journal from Oregon focused on the poetry of place.